Six Hats and a Box

by William Baxley
illustrated by Vicki Shirey

Practice Decodable 25

I0805986

McGraw Hill Education

Bothell, WA • Chicago, IL • Columbus, OH • New York, NY

MHEonline.com

Send all inquiries to:
McGraw-Hill Education
8787 Orion Place
Columbus, OH 43240

ISBN: 978-0-02-144788-6
MHID: 0-02-144788-8

Printed in the United States of America.

7 8 9 CTM 23

A Hat Box

When Dad got six hats, Max got a box.

A Bus

A box can be a bus for a boy.
Max had pens and made a bus.

He cut out holes.

That is when Dad came.

Big Hats

The hats did not fit Dad!

They must go in that box!

The boy and dad smiled.
They went out for a box!